ABIDING-
HONESTY IN RELATIONSHIP

BY
NEVA COYLE

SERIES III

in the OVEREATERS VICTORIOUS program
for Christian weight-loss

BETHANY HOUSE PUBLISHERS
MINNEAPOLIS, MINNESOTA 55438
A Division of Bethany Fellowship, Inc.

Tape Albums and Study Guides by Neva Coyle:

The study guides come with the tape albums but may also be ordered separately.

A Seminar on Living Free, a recording of her seminar in which she shares the principles that have helped her break free from a life of misery and self-satisfaction (four cassettes)
Living Free Study Guide, to accompany the tape album

Free To Be Thin (seven cassettes) Victory, Weight-loss, Deliverance
Free To Be Thin Study Guide No. 1, Getting Started, to be used with the book by the same title, and/or the tape album

Discipline (four cassettes) A Program for Spiritual Fitness
Free To Be Thin Study Guide No. 2, Discipline, to be used with the book by the same title, and/or the tape album

Abiding (four cassettes) Honesty in Relationships
Abiding Study Guide

Freedom (four cassettes) Escape from the Ordinary
Freedom Study Guide

Diligence (four cassettes) Overcoming Discouragement
Diligence Study Guide

Obedience (four cassettes) Developing a Listening Heart
Obedience Study Guide

Free To Be Thin Aerobics, available in LP record album with booklet or cassette tape album with booklet.

Abiding
Neva Coyle

Published by Bethany Fellowship, Inc.
6820 Auto Club Road, Minneapolis, Minnesota 55438

Printed in the United States of America

A NOTE FROM NEVA

In this third series of lessons, I expect that you will come to know more fully the depth of the relationship God offers to His children. The title, "Abiding," comes from a word study that I did a while back, seeking to be a doer of the Word from John 15:1-10. What does it actually mean to "abide"?

Abide takes on a broad meaning when one looks it up in a dictionary, exploring all the many facets of this interesting word. Look at what I found:

Endurance, permanence, continuance in action,
Keeping the ball rolling, presence, rest and stillness,
Expectation

All these are implied in "abiding." When we apply all these words to our relationship to Jesus Christ and God, our Father, we find a relationship worth exploring to its fullest. Look with me now, into the lessons based on the Psalms, written to the person for whom overeating has been a real problem.

My prayer for you in this series is that in taking a closer look at the provision God has made for us in His Word, you will find a newness, a freshness and excitement, searching out the unsearchable riches we have in Christ Jesus.

Because of Jesus,

Neva Coyle

BEFORE YOU BEGIN

This is the third series of lessons, and to receive full benefit it should be studied in sequence. If you have not already studied *Free To Be Thin*, we would recommend that you begin there.

Each study guide is furnished with Basic Journal Sheets to guide you in your daily quiet time. Follow this guideline and use it as preparation for the lesson, then proceed to the lesson and, finally, listen to the teaching tape. This sequence in preparation will enable you to receive the fullest measure God intends for you.

For Your Preparation—Basic Journal Sheet

1ST DAY ________ TIME ____ REFERENCE: Psalm 9:1-12 God is our refuge

God is impressing on me: | I've shared with the Lord . . .

Thoughts I'm having today: ________

2ND DAY ________ TIME ____ REFERENCE: Heb. 1:10-12 God is always there

God is impressing on me: | I've shared with the Lord . . .

Thoughts I'm having today: ________

3RD DAY ________ TIME ____ REFERENCE: Psalm 102:27-28 God does not change

God is impressing on me: | I've shared with the Lord . . .

Thoughts I'm having today: ________

4TH DAY ________ TIME ____ REFERENCE: Psalm 42 God will sustain me

God is impressing on me: | I've shared with the Lord . . .

Thoughts I'm having today: ____________________

5TH DAY ________ TIME ____ REFERENCE: Ps. 12:5-7 God will keep His promises

God is impressing on me: | I've shared with the Lord . . .

Thoughts I'm having today: ____________________

6TH DAY ________ TIME ____ REFERENCE: Ps. 3:2-4; 6:9 God hears & answers

God is impressing on me: | I've shared with the Lord . . .

Thoughts I'm having today: ____________________

7TH DAY _______ TIME ____ REFERENCE: Ps. 9:11-12 God is worthy of our praise

God is impressing on me:

I've shared with the Lord . . .

- -

Thoughts I'm having today: ____

WEEKLY EVALUATION

What principles has the Lord taught me this week? ____________________

How can I be more faithful in honoring the Lord next week? ______________

What changes am I seeing in my attitude towards:

Food? ____

God? ____

Others? ______________________________________

LESSON ONE

AFFLICTION AND OPPRESSION (BLESSING IN DISGUISE?)

Psalm 9:9

"The Lord will be a refuge and a high tower for the oppressed, a refuge and a stronghold in times of trouble."

Vs. 12:

" . . . He does not forget the cry of the afflicted." AMP

Define "afflicted": ______________________________

____

____

____

Is FAT an affliction for you? ________ How? ______________________________

____

____

Define "oppression" or "oppressed" or "oppressive": ______________________________

____

____

____

____

Is being overweight oppressive to you? ______ Is overeating oppressive to you? ______

Why? ______________________________

____

____

NOW THAT WE HAVE ESTABLISHED THAT WE ARE EITHER OPPRESSED OR AFFLICTED AS OVERWEIGHT AND OVEREATING CHRISTIANS, LET'S LOOK AT THE REST OF THE 9TH VERSE OF PSALM 9:

"The Lord will be a stronghold for the oppressed. . . . "

What is a stronghold? ______________________________

____

Look at "strong-hold" as two different words, and then add the meanings together:

STRONG	HOLD
______________	______________
______________	______________
______________	______________
______________	______________
______________	______________

In your own words, define "stronghold": ______________________________

____

____

When thinking of God as our stronghold, how do these definitions apply to our temptations with food?

____

____

____

Make a list of the times you need a stronghold the most:

____

____

____

Read Psalm 9:10

"And those who know Thy ________ will put their ________ in Thee, for Thou, O Lord, hast not ________________ those who ________________ Thee."

How do we run into the stronghold (God) for safety? ________________________

____

Verse 12 says, *"He does not forget the cry of the afflicted."*

Who is the afflicted? ____________ Are you? __________

A PROMISE:

Psalm 12:5 (NAS): *"Because of the devastation of the afflicted, because of the groaning of the needy, now I will arise, says the Lord, I will set him in the safety for which he longs."*

IS THAT AN ANSWER TO YOUR PRAYER?

ASSIGNMENT:

1. Use the Basic Journal Sheet. Read scriptures daily and enter notes in your journal.
2. Continue recording food intake and calories on Calorie Account Sheet.
3. Plan your menu for at least one whole day—in advance.
4. Call an OV friend at the urging of the Holy Spirit.
5. Ask God to tell you what size dress/suit you will wear at your goal weight and then start window shopping in order to get a glimpse of what a miracle God is doing in your body.
6. Set a goal for the week: "My goal for this week (date) ________________________ is: ____

   ____

For Your Preparation—Basic Journal Sheet

1ST DAY ________ TIME ____ REFERENCE: Ps. 17:1-5

God is impressing on me: | I've shared with the Lord . . .

Thoughts I'm having today: ____________________

2ND DAY ________ TIME ____ REFERENCE: Ps. 17:6-17

God is impressing on me: | I've shared with the Lord . . .

Thoughts I'm having today: ____________________

3RD DAY ________ TIME ____ REFERENCE: Ps. 18:1-3

God is impressing on me: | I've shared with the Lord . . .

Thoughts I'm having today: ____________________

4TH DAY ______ TIME ____ REFERENCE: Ps. 107:5-9

God is impressing on me: | I've shared with the Lord . . .

Thoughts I'm having today: ______

5TH DAY ______ TIME ____ REFERENCE: Ps. 145:17-18

God is impressing on me: | I've shared with the Lord . . .

Thoughts I'm having today: ______

6TH DAY ______ TIME ____ REFERENCE: Ps. 107:13 & 19-20

God is impressing on me: | I've shared with the Lord . . .

Thoughts I'm having today: ______

7TH DAY ______ TIME ____ REFERENCE: Ps. 120:1 (Memorize)

God is impressing on me:

I've shared with the Lord . . .

Thoughts I'm having today: ______________________________

WEEKLY EVALUATION

What principles has the Lord taught me this week? ______________________________

How can I be more faithful in honoring the Lord next week? ______________________________

What changes am I seeing in my attitude towards:

Food? ______________________________

God? ______________________________

Others? ______________________________

LESSON TWO

"CRYING UNTO THE LORD"

Crying unto the Lord as recorded in the scriptures is not having a pity party and expecting God to sympathize with His "spoiled" children. It is, instead, an attitude of prayer that is typified by prayer earnestly coming from our deepest need.

Psalm 17:1-5

" . . . *give heed to my cry*" is found in the first verse of this precious Psalm.

Define "cry" from a dictionary: ____

With this definition in mind, express in your own words what a cry to the Lord is: ______

How does a cry to the Lord differ from other kinds of prayers? For example: a thanksgiving prayer comes from a grateful heart for God's activity and involvement in our lives (salvation, blessings, healing, miracles, etc.). Prayers of praise come from an awareness of who God is (Holy Father, Creator, Savior, Comforter).

Crying to the Lord comes from an awareness of: ________________________________

Have you ever had an experience of crying to the Lord? _________________________

Look at Psalm 107:5-9

What was their trouble (verse 5)? ______________________________________

Can you relate to their need? ________

What did God do for them (verses 6-7)? ___________________________________

What kind of prayer was offered to God next (verse 8)? _________________________

Why (verse 9)? ____

Notice that when the prayer was because of their hunger, the Lord answered with the appropriate satisfaction. God's answer to our prayers are always appropriate to our need.

Go back to Psalm 17:1

" . . . give ear to my prayer which is not from deceitful lips."

It is important that when we call upon the Lord we call upon Him in the entirety of the truth. When we are conscious of praying in truth, prayers of "Lord, I can't," sometimes become "Lord, I won't." That is an important step of honesty toward truth. "Lord, I won't," can then become "Lord, I will, with Your help."

What else do we as overeaters think of when we think of deceitful lips? ____________________

____

How about the double meaning for us in verse 3?

"I have purposed that my mouth will not transgress."

____

____

____

Psalm 145:17-18

When we call or cry unto the Lord, it is essential that we call upon His name in ____________.

Give a dictionary definition of "truth": ____________________

____

____

____

HOW DOES THIS ENTIRE "PRINCIPLE OF CRYING UNTO THE LORD IN TRUTH" HELP US IN OUR EATING PLAN? ____________________

____

____

____

____

HOW DOES THIS "PRINCIPLE" APPLY TO OUR CONFESSIONS TO THE LORD?

____

____

____

Memorize Psalm 120:1

"In my trouble I cried to the Lord, and He answered me."

Learn to use this verse OUT LOUD when faced with temptation.

HE *WILL* ANSWER!

ASSIGNMENT:

1. Continue recording food intake and calories on a Calorie Account Sheet.
2. Use the Basic Journal Sheet. Use a supplementary spiral or binder to make additional entries in your journal, noting other scripture references especially helpful in your food battle, your daily calories and insight about food selections.

3. List areas of your life in which you need to be more truthful with:
   a. God ______________________________
   b. Yourself ______________________________
   c. Others ______________________________
4. Plan your menu in advance for at least two days this week. Call an OV friend or supportive prayer partner this week.
5. Set a goal for the week.
   a. __________ calories per day.
   b. __________ minutes with God each day.
   c. Other: ______________________________
   ____
   ____

Dear God,

I would like to lose __________ pounds during this series of lessons. Would You please help me? Tell me what to do to be in a position of obedience to You. I give You my appetite and my obedience.

______________________________ ______________
(signed) (date)

For Your Preparation—Basic Journal Sheet

1ST DAY ________ TIME ____ REFERENCE: Ps. 18:20-24

God is impressing on me:

I've shared with the Lord . . .

Thoughts I'm having today: ________________________________

____

____

____

2ND DAY ________ TIME ____ REFERENCE: Isaiah 64:4-5

God is impressing on me:

I've shared with the Lord . . .

Thoughts I'm having today: ________________________________

____

____

____

3RD DAY ________ TIME ____ REFERENCE: Isaiah 25:6-9

God is impressing on me:

I've shared with the Lord . . .

Thoughts I'm having today: ________________________________

____

____

____

4TH DAY _______ TIME ____ REFERENCE: Isaiah 56:1-5

God is impressing on me:

I've shared with the Lord . . .

Thoughts I'm having today: ____________________

5TH DAY _______ TIME ____ REFERENCE: Romans 6:11-23

God is impressing on me:

I've shared with the Lord . . .

Thoughts I'm having today: ____________________

6TH DAY _______ TIME ____ REFERENCE: Romans 14:17

God is impressing on me:

I've shared with the Lord . . .

Thoughts I'm having today: ____________________

7TH DAY ______ TIME ____ REFERENCE: II Cor. 5:15-21

God is impressing on me:	I've shared with the Lord . . .

- -

Thoughts I'm having today: ______________________________

____

____

____

WEEKLY EVALUATION

What principles has the Lord taught me this week? ______________________________

____

How can I be more faithful in honoring the Lord next week? ______________________________

____

What changes am I seeing in my attitude towards:

Food? ______________________________

God? ______________________________

Others? ______________________________

LESSON THREE

TRUTH

Part 1

Psalm 18:20-24

IN THE LAST LESSON WE ESTABLISHED THE NEED FOR TRUTH, ABSOLUTE TRUTH, IN ITS ENTIRETY. IN THIS LESSON WE SHALL DISCOVER THROUGH SCRIPTURE THAT TRUTH IS A PREREQUISITE TO VICTORY.

Psalm 18:20

"The Lord has __________ me according to my ________________."

Define "reward": ____

____

____

Two key words in the above scripture are related to each other very closely. The kind of reward depends on the kind or quality of righteousness.

Read Isaiah 64:4-6

God meets the person who __________ in doing righteousness. But as we go on sinning and leading independent, smug lives, all our righteous deeds are as ________________ __________.

The hope of being rewarded for righteousness that is like filthy rags is not too exciting, is it?

Romans 6:11-23

Verse 11: *"Consider yourselves ____________ to sin but ____________ to God."*
Verse 12: *"Do not let sin reign in your mortal body that you should ____________ its ________________."*

Is overeating obeying the lusts of the body? __________

Verse 16: *"You are the __________________ of the one whom you ________________."*

Sin results in ____________, but obedience results in _____________.
What does "*obedient from the heart*" (verse 17) mean to you? ________________

____

____

Verse 18: *"Having been ____________ from ____________ you became ____________ to ________________."*

Verse 19: When we are slaves to impurity and to lawlessness, it results in ____________. Does overeating fit that pattern? __________ When we become slaves to righteousness, it results in ________________.

Verse 22: What is the outcome of sanctification? ______________________

____

According to this, is the lawless life of overindulgence and overeating serious? ______

____

Verse 23: What is the wages of sin? ______________________

But in Jesus, the free gift of God is ______________ ________

Paraphrase Romans 14:17 in your own words: ______________________

____

____

Read II Corinthians 5:15-21

Verse 20: How can you be reconciled to God in your eating habits? ____________

____

____

Verse 21:

"He made Him (who? ______________) who knew no sin to be sin on ____________ behalf, that ____________ might become ______________________ ____ ."

NOW OUR RIGHTEOUSNESS IS NO LONGER AS FILTHY RAGS—BUT GLORIOUS AND PURE AS JESUS. NOW PSALM 18:20 HOLDS NEW HOPE! READ IT AGAIN . Next week: "The Cleanness of My Hands."

ASSIGNMENT:

1. Continue recording in journal daily. Use the Basic Journal Sheet.
   a. Record other scripture references you read especially helpful in your food battle.
   b. Note your total food intake and calories.
2. Continue recording food intake and calories on Calorie Account Sheet. Stay within calorie limit.
3. Set goals for the coming week.
4. Memorize II Cor. 5:21 and use it when you are tempted.
5. Try planning your menu several days in advance this week.
6. Call an OV friend or prayer partner this week.

For Your Preparation—Basic Journal Sheet

1ST DAY _______ TIME ____ REFERENCE: Ps. 18:20-24

God is impressing on me: | I've shared with the Lord . . .

Thoughts I'm having today: ____________________

2ND DAY _______ TIME ____ REFERENCE: Ps. 7

God is impressing on me: | I've shared with the Lord . . .

Thoughts I'm having today: ____________________

3RD DAY _______ TIME ____ REFERENCE: Ps. 24:1-6

God is impressing on me: | I've shared with the Lord . . .

Thoughts I'm having today: ____________________

4TH DAY ______ TIME ___ REFERENCE: Ps. 37:23-34

God is impressing on me:

I've shared with the Lord . . .

Thoughts I'm having today: ______

5TH DAY ______ TIME ___ REFERENCE: Ps. 119:33-40

God is impressing on me:

I've shared with the Lord . . .

Thoughts I'm having today: ______

6TH DAY ______ TIME ___ REFERENCE: Ps. 18:30-36

God is impressing on me:

I've shared with the Lord . . .

Thoughts I'm having today: ______

7TH DAY ________ TIME ____ REFERENCE: Ps. 18:20-24 (Repeat)

God is impressing on me:	I've shared with the Lord . . .

Thoughts I'm having today: ____

____

____

____

WEEKLY EVALUATION

What principles has the Lord taught me this week? ______________________

____

How can I be more faithful in honoring the Lord next week? ______________

____

What changes am I seeing in my attitude towards:

Food? ____

God? ____

Others? ____

LESSON FOUR

TRUTH

Part 2

Psalm 18:20-24

What does the "*cleanness of my hands*" mean to you? ______________________________

____

____

Psalm 18 describes cleanness of hands:

Verse 21: "*I have* ____ "

Verse 21: " *I have not* ______________________ ______________________

______________________________ "

Verse 22: "*All His* __________________________ *were* ______________________

"*I did not* ____

Verse 23: "*I was also* ____

And I ____."

List several ways the above truth applies to your eating habits and eating plan.

1. ____

2. ____

3. ____

4. ____

5. ____

Read I John 1:9

"*If we* ____________________ *our* ______________, *He is faithful and righteous to* ____________________ *our sins and to* ____________________ *us from all* ____________________________________."

PRAISE GOD!

Psalm 18:24

"*Therefore the Lord has recompensed me according to my* ______________________________."

Which is: (II Cor. 5:21)

"*The* ____________________ *of God in* ________________ *(*________________*)*"

He requires righteousness—He provides righteousness—through __________ (I John 1:9).

"*According to the cleanness of my hands.*"

TRUTH IS IMPORTANT! SO IMPORTANT BECAUSE IT IS THE FIRST STEP TOWARD VICTORY! LET'S GET OUR RELATIONSHIP WITH GOD ON AN "ABSOLUTELY HONEST" BASIS.

ASSIGNMENT:

1. Continue having a daily quiet time with the Lord, recording in your journal. Use the Basic Journal Sheet and make additional entries in your supplemental journal notebook. Note scriptures that speak to you regarding your eating habits.
2. Record your food intake on a Calorie Account Sheet. Be truthful!
3. Plan your menus for three days in advance this week and stick to it.
4. Call an OV friend or prayer partner this week.
5. Set a goal for this week:
   a. __________ calories per day.
   b. __________minutes with God each day.
   c. Other ____
   ____
   ____
6. My progress toward my weight-loss goal for this series of lessons: __________ lost, __________ to go.

For Your Preparation—Basic Journal Sheet

1ST DAY ________ TIME ____ REFERENCE: Ps. 18:25-29

God is impressing on me: | I've shared with the Lord . . .

Thoughts I'm having today: ____________________

2ND DAY ________ TIME ____ REFERENCE: Matt. 5:7, Luke 6:36

God is impressing on me: | I've shared with the Lord . . .

Thoughts I'm having today: ____________________

3RD DAY ________ TIME ____ REFERENCE: Luke 6:31, Matt. 6:12-15

God is impressing on me: | I've shared with the Lord . . .

Thoughts I'm having today: ____________________

4TH DAY ______ TIME ____ REFERENCE: Matt. 18:23-25

God is impressing on me: | I've shared with the Lord . . .

Thoughts I'm having today: ______

5TH DAY ______ TIME ____ REFERENCE: Romans 8:5-11

God is impressing on me: | I've shared with the Lord . . .

Thoughts I'm having today: ______

6TH DAY ______ TIME ____ REFERENCE: Gal. 5:16-25

God is impressing on me: | I've shared with the Lord . . .

Thoughts I'm having today: ______

7TH DAY _______ TIME ____ REFERENCE: Gal. 6:7-9, Rom. 8:7-8

God is impressing on me: | I've shared with the Lord . . .

Thoughts I'm having today: ______________________________

____

____

____

WEEKLY EVALUATION

What principles has the Lord taught me this week? ______________________________

____

How can I be more faithful in honoring the Lord next week? ______________________________

____

What changes am I seeing in my attitude towards:

Food? ______________________________

God? ______________________________

Others? ______________________________

LESSON FIVE

RELATIONSHIP

Part 1

IN THE LAST LESSON WE DISCUSSED THE IMPORTANCE OF BEING ENTIRELY HONEST AND TRUTHFUL IN OUR EATING HABITS AS WELL AS IN EVERY OTHER AREA OF OUR LIVES WITH GOD.

How have you incorporated the principle of truth into your life in this last week? ________

____

____

Specifically, how have you applied the last lesson to your eating plan? ____________

____

____

Psalm 18:25-29

Notice that as "truth" is discussed in Psalm 18:20-24, there is a "relationship" revealed in verses 25-29. Let's examine this relationship, remembering that "truth" as the foundation for a relationship is covered first, then the relationship.

Verse 25: *"With the kind, Thou dost show Thyself to be kind."*

Matt. 5:7: *"____________________ are the merciful for they shall ________ ____________________."*

Luke 6:36: *"Be ________________ as ____________________ is ____________________."*

Define "mercy": ____

____

____

____

Mercy is an act. But watch out! Mercy can be handled cruelly. Our attitude must be one of kindness.

Define "kind" (adjective): ____________________________________

____

____

____

For example, take this situation: A young family is visiting your house for Sunday dinner.

All goes well until after dinner when the young visiting mother insists upon helping clean up the dishes. In the course of cleaning up and washing and drying the dishes, she drops and breaks an antique relish plate. Let's look at two responses:

1. You shriek and then start carefully picking up the pieces and deposit the whole dish in the trash. You can tell she is terribly upset by what she has done. You tell her the history of the plate, how it's been in your husband's family for three generations, and so on. Then you tell her the dollar value of the plate and now it's her turn to shriek. "Oh, please," she cries, "I must pay for it or try to replace it for you." "It isn't replaceable," you say, "and it wouldn't be the same anyway. Just forget it."

Mercy has been shown, but yet something is lacking. What would happen if we added kindness?

2. You are alarmed but you ask, "Are you all right? Did you cut yourself?" "No," she replies, "I'm okay, but I feel terrible about the dish." "Listen, Mary, the Bible says that where our heart is, our treasure is also; and my heart and treasure is in Christ. This dish is a material blessing, and our friendship is a spiritual blessing. I know you feel bad. I also know it was an accident. I forgive you. Now let's clean up the glass slivers before they are trampled by some little toes.

Two things are added: ____________________ and ____________________.

What conditions for relationship are suggested in these passages?

Luke 6:31 ____

Matt. 6:12-15 ____

Matt. 18:23-35 ____

Do you want God to be merciful, kind and forigiving to you? __________ Then what is your responsibility concerning others?

Let's pray and ask God to reveal to us if we have unkindness or unforgiveness toward anyone.

If God is revealing someone to you, won't you purpose to forgive him and make it right with him? Is the price of not receiving forgiveness for our sins and shortcomings worth it?

Psalm 18:25b:

"With the blameless thou dost show thyself blameless."

A blameless person is not the one who never does anything wrong, but rather a person who takes the responsibility for his own behavior and then the appropriate action.

Example: A person eats all the gooey hot dishes and desserts at a church supper. A blameless person does not blame the church but accepts the responsibility for the disobedience and gluttony and then confesses it to God and receives the forgiveness for the sin. And it's done! I don't blame the church; I "fess up" and take the responsibility myself. Then God forgives, and afterwards—no blame. God reveals himself as blameless!

Psalm 18:26:

"With the pure Thou dost show Thyself to be pure."

Define "pure": ____

____

____

Do you consider yourself pure when you are overeating?

Define "defiled": ____

____

____

Remember: IT IS NOT THE FOOD THAT DEFILES (SPIRITUALLY SPEAKING), BUT THE ACT OF DISOBEDIENCE—OF EATING SOMETHING WE ARE NOT SUPPOSED TO.

If to the pure God reveals His purity, then the defiled cannot see the purity of God's will and ways.

What do these passages have to say about the law of the Spirit of life?

Rom. 8:5-11 ______________________________

Gal. 5:16-25 ______________________________

Gal. 6:7-9 ______________________________

So then, if a person sows purity, he will reap *purity*!

Make a list of the ways you can "sow" purity, directly relating this list to your eating habits:

____

____

____

____

____

Psalm 18:26b

". . . and with the crooked, Thou dost show Thyself astute."

Define "astute": ______________________________

____

____

____

Read Romans 8:7-8

Again, the law of sowing and reaping. It is one of God's laws—just like the law of gravity. If we live "crooked" lives, we see God as "astute." If you drop an orange from a fifty-story window, it will splatter.

How do you want to see God? As astute ________ or pure ________

What do you have to do this week to avail yourself of God's purity? (Review your "purity" list.) ______________________________

____

____

____

ASSIGNMENT:

1. Use the Basic Journal Sheet. Read scriptures daily and enter notes in your journal.
2. Record your food intake on a Calorie Account Sheet. Make note of your attitude when eating.
3. Use your journal to record your feelings and frustrations, your defeats and victories.
4. Plan four days of advance menus.
5. Be sure to call your OV friend or prayer partner this week.
6. Set goals that reflect your desire to deepen your relationship with God.

For Your Preparation—Basic Journal Sheet

1ST DAY ________ TIME ____ REFERENCE: Ps. 18:25-29

God is impressing on me: | I've shared with the Lord . . .

Thoughts I'm having today: ________________

2ND DAY ________ TIME ____ REFERENCE: I Cor. 10:12

God is impressing on me: | I've shared with the Lord . . .

Thoughts I'm having today: ________________

3RD DAY ________ TIME ____ REFERENCE: Ps. 40:1-3

God is impressing on me: | I've shared with the Lord . . .

Thoughts I'm having today: ________________

4TH DAY ______ TIME ____ REFERENCE: Ps. 107:1&2

God is impressing on me:

I've shared with the Lord . . .

Thoughts I'm having today: ____________________

5TH DAY ______ TIME ____ REFERENCE: Ps. 119:11 and 112

God is impressing on me:

I've shared with the Lord . . .

Thoughts I'm having today: ____________________

6TH DAY ______ TIME ____ REFERENCE: Ps. 18:28

God is impressing on me:

I've shared with the Lord . . .

Thoughts I'm having today: ____________________

7TH DAY ______ TIME ____ REFERENCE: Prov. 6:23, Isa. 60:19-20

God is impressing on me: | I've shared with the Lord . . .

Thoughts I'm having today: ______

WEEKLY EVALUATION

What principles has the Lord taught me this week? ______

How can I be more faithful in honoring the Lord next week? ______

What changes am I seeing in my attitude towards:

Food? ______

God? ______

Others? ______

LESSON SIX

RELATIONSHIP

Part 2

Psalm 18:27

"For Thou dost save an afflicted people. But haughty eyes Thou dost abase."

A few lessons ago we defined "afflicted." What does it mean?

____

____

____

Is your fat an affliction to you? __________

Psalm 18:27

"For Thou (God) dost __________ an afflicted people."

THAT PROMISE IS FOR YOU!

How is God going to save you from a fat life? ____________________________________

____

____

____

Psalm 18:27b

"But ________________ eyes Thou dost ________________."

Define "haughty": ____

____

____

Define "abase": ____

____

____

Read I Corinthians 10:12

"Therefore let him ________ __________ _______ ____________ take heed __________ ____________ ______________."

How can we avoid pride as we lose weight?

Ps. 40:1-3 ____

Ps. 107:1 ____

Ps. 107:2 ____

Ps. 119:11 ____

Ps. 119:112 ____

Other scripture verses you have:

______________ ____

______________ ____

______________ ____

Psalm 18:28

"For Thou dost light my lamp."

How do these verses describe the light we shall have?

Proverbs 6:23 ______________________________

____

Isaiah 60:19-20 ______________________________

____

Psalms 18:28b

"The Lord my God illumines my darkness."

Before, I was in darkness concerning my weight. I didn't know how to eat. I didn't know how to get loose from my addictions to food. But God came and "lit" my lamp by saving me and filling me with His Holy Spirit. Then God "illumines my darkness" with His Word. He is teaching me what to eat, when to eat and how much to eat.

Does the Lord *really* save afflicted people? Yes, PRAISE HIS NAME! He is doing it for me! He is doing it for you!

I can shout Psalm 18:29, "*For by Thee I can run upon a troop*" (whether it be an army of calories camped on a family holiday table, a wedding reception or church supper), "*and by my God I can leap over a wall.*"

FREE OF FAT! LIMBER AND SUPPLE—HEALTHY AND THIN—PRAISE GOD! WE HAVE A RELATIONSHIP!

Comments: ______________________________

____

____

____

____

ASSIGNMENT:

1. Have a daily quiet time with the Lord, recording in your journal. Use both the Basic Journal Sheet and your supplemental journal.
2. Record your food intake on a Calorie Account Sheet.
3. Make note of your feelings (frustrations and victories) when you eat and also when you are able to give up a certain food.
4. Plan menus in advance. Set goals for the week.
5. Call an OV friend or prayer partner. (Pursue a relationship.)

NOTE:

Have you ordered the next series? Now would be a good time if you plan to go on. Use the form in the back of the book to receive a current price list.

For Your Preparation—Basic Journal Sheet

1ST DAY ______ TIME ____ REFERENCE: Ps. 18:30-36

God is impressing on me:	I've shared with the Lord . . .

Thoughts I'm having today: ______________________

2ND DAY ______ TIME ____ REFERENCE: Eph. 5:6-17

God is impressing on me:	I've shared with the Lord . . .

Thoughts I'm having today: ______________________

3RD DAY ______ TIME ____ REFERENCE: Romans 12:2

God is impressing on me:	I've shared with the Lord . . .

Thoughts I'm having today: ______________________

4TH DAY _______ TIME ___ REFERENCE: Titus 3:5

God is impressing on me: | I've shared with the Lord . . .

Thoughts I'm having today: ________________

5TH DAY _______ TIME ___ REFERENCE: Rom. 7:15-25

God is impressing on me: | I've shared with the Lord . . .

Thoughts I'm having today: ________________

6TH DAY _______ TIME ___ REFERENCE: Review Ps. 18:30-36

God is impressing on me: | I've shared with the Lord . . .

Thoughts I'm having today: ________________

'TH DAY ______ TIME ____ REFERENCE: Review Ps. 18:30; "God's Will Today" Chart

}od is impressing on me:

I've shared with the Lord . . .

Thoughts I'm having today: ______________________________

____

____

____

WEEKLY EVALUATION

What principles has the Lord taught me this week? ______________________________

____

How can I be more faithful in honoring the Lord next week? ______________________________

____

What changes am I seeing in my attitude towards:

Food? ______________________________

God? ______________________________

Others? ______________________________

LESSON SEVEN

VICTORY

Part 1

Psalm 18:30

"As for God, His way is blameless; the word of the Lord is tried, He is a shield to all who take refuge in Him."

God's way . . .

Psalm 119:1 (AMP)

"Blessed, happy, fortunate (to be envied) are the undefiled—the upright, truly sincere and blameless—in the way *(of the revealed will of God); who walk—that is, order their conduct and conversation—in (the whole of God's revealed will) the law of the Lord."*

God expects us to walk *only* in as much of His will as He has revealed to us. *BUT*, God expects us to walk *totally* in as much as He has revealed to us.

Read Ephesians 5:6-17

Vs. 10 (AMP): *"And try to learn (in your experience) what is pleasing to the Lord; (let your lives be constant) proofs of what is acceptable to Him."*

List some of the ways you can do that:

____

____

____

____

Vs. 15:

"Therefore be careful how you walk."

What does this mean to you in the area of your food program?

____

____

____

Verse 17:

" . . . understand what the will of the Lord is."

HOW DO WE UNDERSTAND THE WILL OF THE LORD?

Romans 12:2:

1. Break the ties of __________ __________.
2. Be ________________ by the ____________________ of you ________________.

Titus 3:5

3. According to ________________. Done by ________________ __________

IOW DOES THE HOLY SPIRIT LEAD US INTO GOD'S WILL?

I Tim. 3:16-17 1. Through the illumination of scripture.
Ephesians 5:10 2. By experience.
Ephesians 5:13 3. By conviction.
Ephesians 5:14 4. By revelation.

PERHAPS YOU FIND YOURSELF IN A PREDICAMENT LIKE PAUL'S IN ROMANS :15-25 (LB)

"We want to do what is right, we only seem to do what is wrong. Where does the trouble lie?"

THE BIBLE SAYS THAT CHRIST HAS ALREADY MADE US FREE SO WE CAN'T BLAME HIM. *HE* IS PERFECT! *WE* ARE *NOT* PERFECT! AS A RECEIVER, WE STILL HAVE SOME "WIRES CROSSED" SOMEWHERE. LET US PURPOSE, BEFORE GOD, TO ALLOW THE HOLY SPIRIT TO LEAD US INTO HIS PERFECT WILL—HIS WAY! (PSALM 18:30)

HAS THE LORD REVEALED A NEW TRUTH TO YOU IN THIS LESSON? WHAT IS IT?

____

____

____

NOW PRAISE GOD FOR WHAT YOU HAVE LEARNED. REMEMBER WITH EVERY MEASURE OF GOD'S REVEALED WILL COMES THE RESPONSIBILITY TO WALK IN IT! Psalm 18:30b

". . . He is a shield to all who take refuge in Him."

HE WANTS TO PROTECT US! HE WANTS TO HOLD US IN A PLACE OF SAFETY—BUT WE MUST TAKE REFUGE IN HIM!

ASSIGNMENT:

1. Have a daily quiet time with the Lord, recording in your journal. Use both the Basic Journal Sheet and your supplementary notebook.
2. Record your food intake on a Calorie Account Sheet.
3. Plan your menus ahead. Introduce a new food.
4. Call an OV friend or prayer partner this week.
5. Set goal for week: ______________________________

____

____

LESSON EIGHT

For Your Preparation—Basic Journal Sheet

1ST DAY ________ TIME ____ REFERENCE: Review Ps. 18:30-36

God is impressing on me: | I've shared with the Lord . . .

Thoughts I'm having today: ____

2ND DAY ________ TIME ____ REFERENCE: Ps. 18:31-32

God is impressing on me: | I've shared with the Lord . . .

Thoughts I'm having today: ____

3RD DAY ________ TIME ____ REFERENCE: Ps. 18:33-36

God is impressing on me: | I've shared with the Lord . . .

Thoughts I'm having today: ____

4TH DAY _______ TIME ____ REFERENCE: Ps. 18:37-50

God is impressing on me: | I've shared with the Lord . . .

Thoughts I'm having today: ________________________________

5TH DAY _______ TIME ____ REFERENCE: Review Ps. 18:20-24

God is impressing on me: | I've shared with the Lord . . .

Thoughts I'm having today: ________________________________

6TH DAY _______ TIME ____ REFERENCE: Psalm 18:25-29

God is impressing on me: | I've shared with the Lord . . .

Thoughts I'm having today: ________________________________

7TH DAY ________ TIME ____ REFERENCE: Review & meditate Ps. 18:30-36

God is impressing on me:

I've shared with the Lord . . .

Thoughts I'm having today: ____

WEEKLY EVALUATION

What principles has the Lord taught me this week? ____________________

How can I be more faithful in honoring the Lord next week? ____________

What changes am I seeing in my attitude towards:

Food? ____________________

God? ____________________

Others? ____________________

LESSON EIGHT

VICTORY

Part 2

Psalm 18:31-32

Who is a God ____________________

Who is a rock? ____________________

Who gives me strength? ____________________

Who makes my way blameless? ____________________

Who gives me the victory in my eating? ____________________

Psalm 18:33-34

"He makes my feet like hind's feet, and sets me upon my high places. He trains my hands for battle, so that my arms can bend a bow of bronze."

Paraphrase these verses to apply to your battle with food:

Psalm 18:35

What does the promise of this verse hold for you?

Psalm 18:36

"Thou dost enlarge my steps under me, and my feet have not slipped."

VICTORY! VICTORY! VICTORY!

Read the remainder of Psalm 18.

Review now: Psalm 18:20-24. See the important element of truth?

Review Psalm 18:25-29. After the truth between God and us is established, a relationship is born!

Review Psalm 18:30-36. It is to those in a truthful relationship to God that He gives victory!

TRUTH . . . RELATIONSHIP . . . VICTORY!!

IN THAT ORDER!

How does this principle of scripture relate to you in the area of overeating?

List other areas you would like to apply this truth:

ASSIGNMENT:

1. Continue to have a daily quiet time with the Lord, recording in your journal.
2. Record your food intake on a Calorie Account Sheet. Be accountable in other areas that need your attention.
3. Include a new recipe this week in your advance menu planning.
4. Call an OV friend or prayer partner this week. (Call when you need someone and call when you can encourage someone.)
5. Evaluate how your relationship with God has changed during this series of lessons. What changes have taken place? What goals have been most helpful?
6. Review each lesson before you go on to the next series: Series IV, FREEDOM: Escape From the Ordinary.

Detach here

- -

For information regarding OVEREATERS VICTORIOUS and for current price lists on other materials, send a business-size, stamped, self-addressed envelope to Overeaters Victorious Inc., P.O. Box 179, Redlands, CA 92373.

If you would like to receive special mailings concerning Overeaters Victorious seminars in your area, fill out the form below. *(Allow four weeks)*

Name ____________________________

Address __________________________

City/State ____________________ Zip ________

Please print or type.